Rabbit Nutrition

(An illustrated guide to edible wild plants)

Text by
VIRGINIA RICHARDSON M.R.C.V.S.

Photographs by
FIONA WEBB

ISBN 1-898015-03-1

Set in 11/15 pt Baskerville,
printed and bound by K.D.S.,
Ipswich, Suffolk, England.

Cover photograph: Herbie the Netherland Dwarf enjoying his daily snack.

CONTENTS

Page No.

Introduction

In order to understand the complex principles of rabbit nutrition it is necessary to appreciate the physiology of the rabbit digestive system. The first part of this system which comes into contact with the food are the teeth. Rabbit incisors can grow between 4-5 inches in a single year, and rely on the constant gnawing and chewing of fibrous foodstuffs to constantly wear them down. It is therefore important to provide hard foods, and also a constant source of fibre for them to chew on a daily basis.

Once the food has been chewed it passes into the stomach where the food is sterilised by the stomach's acid juices, and the food then passes on to the small intestine where the nutrients are absorbed. The ingesta is then divided into small particles of fibre and large particles of fibre. The large particles are processed into the hard pellets, whilst the smaller particles are moved backwards into the caecum for fermentation.

The **caecum** is the fermenting vat of the digestive system, and central to the rabbit's good health. The caecum contains beneficial bacteria which ferment the small fibre particles into volatile fatty acids and B complex vitamins. The result of this caecal fermentation produces caecotrophs, the softer faeces which are eaten by the rabbit once they are passed, to satisfy its vitamin requirement (a process known as caecotrophy). The caecum also contain small amounts of harmful bacteria (*Clostridium spp*) which if they proliferate can produce toxins and cause a fatal diarrhoea, known as enterotoxaemia.

The digestive system runs on **fibre**, the single most important component of the diet. High fibre diets stimulate the fast movement of ingesta through the gut. It is important that the passage of food is relatively fast, as if the gut slows down the build up of hair and ingesta causing a blockage is more common, and if food stays in the caecum for long more harmful bacteria may be able to proliferate. Diets low in large indigestible fibre particles and high in starches and protein may lead to an excess production of caecotrophs, more than the rabbit can reingest and hence the condition of 'sticky bottom'.

The rabbit's requirement for **energy** is met partly by the absorption of the volatile fatty acids produced in the caecum, and also from the starch content of the dry food. Sugary foods are not good for rabbits, as excess sugar and starch may find its way to the caecum, providing fuel for the harmful bacterial to multiply and produce toxins. This is a particularly common problem in young weanlings which begin eating dry food for the first time, they ingest more carbohydrate than the digestive system can cope with ('starch overload') and scouring is common. There is therefore a case for the feeding of astringent plant foods alongside dry food to weanlings, to protect against starch overload, and provide protectant foods against scouring.

The rabbit's **protein** requirements will be met by the dry food, but also from good quality hay and greenstuff. The protein requirement for growth is 16%, and 14% for maintenance.

Minerals and **vitamins** are also important. The vitamin B complex, and vitamin K are provided by coprophagy. If the rabbit is unable to eat its caecal pellets for any reason, e.g. obesity, malocclusion, or whilst scouring, it will need vitamin B supplementation.

The most important minerals are calcium, phosphorus, magnesium, potassium and sodium. The rabbit has a unique calcium metabolism, and this requires special mention. Whereas other species only absorb from the digestive system the amount of calcium they require, the rabbit absorbs all dietary calcium, and excretes the excess in the urine. Calcium binds to phosphorus, so the actual calcium absorbed depends upon the calcium : phosphorus ratio, which should ideally be 2:1. Excess dietary calcium leads to excess urinary calcium, 'sludgy bladder', cystitis, bladder and kidney stones. A restricted calcium diet may lead to poor mineralisation of the teeth. The calcium content of the concentrate ration is in the pellets, and some rabbits become selective and leave the pellets. Only a small amount of dry food should be fed at one time to allow it to be eaten in its entirety before more is offered, so that a balanced diet is being eaten. If bladder stones, or 'sludgy bladder' are a problem attention should be taken of the calcium values of foodstuffs.

Complete Dry Foods

There are many complete dry rations available, completely nutritionally balanced, and formulated to be fed in conjunction with forage (i.e. good hay). It is important that if these are relied upon as the sole food, that the rabbit eats every component of the diet. If the bowl is constantly refilled the rabbit will select only its favourite portions, and its diet will not be properly balanced.

FOREWORD

Ever since I had my first rabbits and guinea-pigs as pets when I was a child I have been interested in the feeding of wild plants. Wild plants can provide a varied and interesting diet, and the majority also have medicinal properties, which I have explored since I qualified as a veterinary surgeon. Most previous texts have relied on the line drawings and written descriptions of plants, and I hope that the colour pictures in this text will make their identification much easier. The idea of this book was born as we walked our dogs together, gathering food for our own rabbits and guinea pigs. As we picked and photographed we built up this collection of plants, and every single one has been tried and tested on our own rabbits. All the plants mentioned are equally suitable for guinea pigs.

V Richardson. MRCVS

References and Further Reading

Bell, F.R. (1971). Greenfoods for Rabbits and Cavies. *Watmoughs Limited. Bradford.*

Fitter, R, Fitter, A, and Blamey, M. (1974). The Wild Flowers of Britain and Northern Europe. *Collins, London.*

Harriman, H. (1991). House Rabbit Handbook. *Drollery Press, USA.*

Okerman, L. (1994). Diseases of Domestic Rabbits. *Blackwell Scientific Publications, Oxford.*

Sandford, J.C. (1996). The Domestic Rabbit. *Blackwell Scientific Publications, Oxford.*

CHAPTER 1
Medical conditions with dietary considerations

There are four main conditions where diet can play an extremely large part. These are in any case of diarrhoea (scouring), the formation of excess caecotrophs ('sticky bottom syndrome'), 'sludgy urine' associated with the formation of bladder stones and dental disease.

Diarrhoea (Scours)

Any case of diarrhoea can be potentially fatal, as it takes so little time for the proliferation of harmful bacteria in the gut to produce toxins and cause enterotoxaemia. Young and weanling animals are particularly susceptible. With any case of diarrhoea **astringent** plants such as Shepherd's Purse and Blackberry leaves should be offered immediately, along with good quality hay. In many instances the treatment of diarrhoea with astringents is more effective than the use of antibiotics, which may actually perpetuate the problem by destroying the beneficial bacteria in the gut further. A probiotic (e.g. Vetark Avipro) should always be given. These contain *Lactobacillus* and *Enterococcus* species which will temporarily repopulate the caecum with beneficial bacteria.

Astringent plants can be fed at all times to prevent scouring, and some of the wild plants may be particularly useful at weaning to protect against scours, and prevent starch overload where the young rabbit ingests excess quantities of dry food. Where astringent plant sources are available too, the dry food intake will be less excessive.

Excess caecotrophs (sticky bottom syndrome)

Some diets, particularly those that are high in protein, low in fibre and high in carbohydrate or sugar will cause the rabbit to produce more caecal faeces than it needs, and hence develop a 'sticky bottom'. If the rabbit is overfed it may lose the urge to practice coprophagy. Caecal faeces may also build up if the rabbit is unable to perform coprophagy, if for example it is overweight, has an excessive dewlap, or has incisor or molar malocclusion (which will make coprophagy uncomfortable).

Dietary reform means changing the rabbit over to a **high** fibre, **low** protein and **low** carbohydrate diet, which actually provides a more natural diet, and one closer to that of their relatives, the wild rabbit. The rabbit's digestive systems works at its best when it has to breakdown plant fibres.

1. There should be unlimited access to good quality grass hay at all times, as the major fibre provider.

2. Dry or pelleted food (which is high in protein and carbohydrate) should be restricted.

3. Processed 'treats' (full of carbohydrate and sugar) should be cut out and replaced with fruit treats.

4. Vegetables and fruit can be slowly introduced from the following list, one at a time. If any item upsets the rabbit it will show diarrhoea 24-48 hours after its introduction, and that fruit or vegetable should be removed from the diet. Once the new regime is fully introduced the rabbit should receive at least ½ cup vegetables/kg body weight daily.

5. Astringent plants such as Blackberry or Raspberry leaves can be introduced immediately, they are a good source of fibre and will not cause diarrhoea. As the majority of edible wild plants are astringent they can eventually all be fed making up the bulk of the ration if vegetables become hard to come by.

Vegetables
Broccoli
Brussel sprouts and sprout tops
Cabbage and cabbage types, spring greens etc.
Carrot and carrot tops
Celery
Clover
Dandelions (leaves and flowers) use sparingly

Kale

Mint

Parsley

Radish Tops

Spinach

Watercress

Fruits

Small amounts of Apple, Peach, Pear, Melon, Pineapple, Plums, Strawberries and Tomatoes can be added or used as 'treats'.

Urinary conditions (stones and 'sludgy bladder')

As these conditions are the result of excess dietary calcium, a transference to a hay and vegetable diet, as mentioned above for 'sticky bottom' is appropriate. Attention must be paid to the calcium value of foods and the vegetables can be divided into good, moderate and poor sources of calcium. Rabbits receiving some dry mix should be fed almost exclusively on moderate or poor sources only (lists 2 & 3). Edible wild plants can be fed ad lib.

Rabbits on no dry mix can have some vegetables from list 1.

If renal dysfunction or kidney stones are an associated problem, vegetables with an asterisk should be avoided due to their high phosphorus content.

1. Good calcium sources	2. Moderate sources	3. Poor calcium sources
Chinese cabbage	Cabbage	Carrots*
Watercress	Strawberries	Cauliflower
Kale	Radish and radish tops	Cucumber
Dandelions		Lettuce
Parsley		Tomato*
Spinach		Bananas*
		Brussels sprouts
		Apples

The vegetable assortment should contain one vitamin A rich vegetable daily, such as carrots, carrot tops, watercress, parsley, broccoli and beetroot greens.

Dental Disease

The causes of incisor and molar malocclusion are multifactorial, one factor is diet. There is a need to provide a diet adequate in calcium and vitamin D (which ensures calcium uptake), and to provide plenty of fibre so that the rabbit has opportunity to chew, and thus wear its teeth down correctly.

At present the best advice to prevent dental disease is as follows:-

1. To offer smaller quantities of dry food to ensure that all components are eaten, and that the rabbit does not selectively leave the pellets.

2. Selective feeders, or rabbits showing obvious calcification defects such as lines in the enamel of the upper incisors can be given supplementation. It is best to give a combined calcium and vitamin D supplement such as Collo-cal D.

3. Hay should be given as a good source of vitamin D.

4. Greenstuff should be given daily, dandelions and clover are good sources of calcium.

5. The rabbit should be allowed access to natural daylight every day.

CHAPTER 2
Edible Wild Plants

There is a vast selection of wild plants to be found throughout the year. This chapter describes each plant, and discusses its useful

Agrimony

properties. Plants should not be collected from areas that may have
been treated with weedkillers or sprays, or from areas soiled by dogs.
Plants from busy roadsides will be covered with exhaust fumes, but
plants from quiet lanes are fine.

The benefits of feeding wild plants is that a varied diet can be fed
throughout the year for free. As the majority of plants are astringent
in action they can be safely fed to stock of all ages. A varied diet should
be fed to the stock from a young age so that they become familiar with
the variety of foodstuffs. If a new plant is fed to an adult for the first
time it may not accept it.

When picking wild plants, the leaves and flowerheads can be picked,
but the plant should not be uprooted. This ensures the plant's regrowth
and future survival.

Agrimony *(Agimonia eupatoria)*

Description:- This is a medium downy perennial with pinnate leaves.
The flowers at 5-8mm diameter, in a spike. It flowers from June-August.
It may grow up to 2 feet high.

Habitat:- Dry grassy places, waste ground and roadside. It favours
lime soils.

Uses:- The whole plant may be fed. Astringent, and has tonic
properties, as it contains iron, vitamins B and K (assists blood clotting)
and essential oils. It is also diuretic.

Avens *(Geum urbanum)*

Description:- This plant is also known as Herb Bennet. A medium
downy perennial with pinnate leaves. The flowers are yellow, 8-15mm
diameter, and when the petals fall off they leave a characteristic brown
centre. It flowers from May-September. All parts of the plant can be
fed, and the leaves are available all year round, making it one of the
most useful plants early in the year.

Avens

Habitat:- Woods and shady places on fertile soils.

Uses:- It is an astringent, and has tonic properties.

Bramble *(Rubus fruticosus)*

Description:- Well known as the common Blackberry, this is a particularly useful plant. Its leaves are available all year round, and the new shoots and leaves that develop in the spring are enjoyed by all the stock. The flowers are 20-30mm diameter, and white or pink. It flowers from May-November. The purple fruits appear from late August onwards. It is the leaves that can be fed.

Habitat:- Woods, scrub, open and waste ground.

Uses:- The leaves are one of the best treatments available for scours, and for simple cases, where the rabbit or cavy appears bright and alert, the withdrawal of all other foods, and the feeding of hay and bramble leaves may be the only measures necessary to correct the condition.

Bramble leaves

Chickweed *(Stellaria media)*

Description:- This is a low, creeping annual, with a line of hairs down the weak round stem. The leaves are oval, the lower leaves are long stalked. The flowers are white, star-like, and 8-10mm diameter, and are present all year. The whole plant can be fed.

Habitat:- Woodlands, and cultivated ground.

Uses:- This plant has no special properties but it is a good source of vitamins and minerals. It is particularly enjoyed by cavies, and provides an interesting variation to the diet. It is an astringent.

Clover *(Trifolium spp)*

Description:- These are well recognised plants, that are members of the pea family. They have dense rounded flower heads, with white or pink flowers. They are perennials and flower from May-October. All parts of the plant can be fed.

Chickweed

Clover

Habitat:- Roadside, grassy fields.

Uses:- They are a good source of protein, and are enjoyed both fresh, and when dried in good quality hay. Clovers are a useful plant to feed during the moult. Clovers also have tonic properties.

Coltsfoot *(Tussilago farfara)*

Description:- It is a low creeping perennial. The flowers appear first, and are single dandelion-like heads on a stem that is covered in purple scales. The plant flowers between February-April. The leaves appear next, and are heart-shaped with pointed teeth, and the underside of the leaf is a silver colour. The leaves grow from the roots only, and may become as much as 12 inches across at their broadest point.

Habitat:- Bare and waste ground, especially in clay soil.

Uses:- The leaves can be fed. The plant has a reputation as a curer of coughs and chest complaints.

Cow Parsnip

Cow Parsnip *(Heracleum sphondylium)*

Description:- This plant is also known as Hogweed. It is a member of the carrot family, and is a large plant which may grow up to 3 metres tall. It has very large leaves, 1-3 pinnate with broad toothed leaflets. The stalks are hairless or roughly hairy. The flowers are white or pink with umbrels up to 20cm across, and it flowers from April-November.

It must not be confused with Hemlock, which is very poisonous. Hemlock has similar flowers, but has fern-like leaves, and has a characteristic stem which is purple spotted. It also has a distinctive fetid odour.

Habitat:- Grassy places, verges, open woodland.

Uses:- Only the leaves should be fed, and the young leaves are the most palatable. The flower heads should not be fed. In the spring this is a succulent plant and useful for nursing does and sows.

Dandelion *(Taraxacum)*

Description:- This plant needs little introduction. It is a particularly common perennial. The yellow flower head are 35-50mm diameter, on hollow stalks, which when picked exude a milky juice. The leaves are in a basal rosette, and broadly toothed. Flowers are present most of the year, especially May-June.

Dandelion

Habitat:- Widespread, gardens, lawns, hedgerows.

Uses:- All parts of the plant can be fed. The leaves are diuretic in action, and have a stimulating effect on the kidney. This plant should be fed sparingly to rabbits, as it also has a laxative action. It is a useful plant to feed if the rabbit is anorexic, or has gastric stasis, to tempt the appetite. Their diuretic action may also help eliminate bladder stones.

Goosegrass *(Galium apaprine)*

Description:- This is also known as Cleavers or 'Sticky weed', as the stems and leaves have numerous down-turning prickles which stick to animal fur and clothing. The fruits are small and green at first, and then turn purple. The fruits are also covered with hooked spines that stick onto clothing. It is a straggling medium tall annual with very small white flowers. It flowers from May-September.

Habitat:- Hedge-banks, fens, disturbed and waste ground.

Uses:- All parts of the plant can be fed. It has an acquired taste, but once the stock become used to it they eat it with relish. It is astringent in action. It is also a diuretic, and may help eliminate bladder stones. It also has tonic properties. Due to the sticky nature of the leaves and fruits it is not a very practical plant to feed to long-haired rabbits e.g. Angoras.

Grass

There are many types of grass, and all can be fed. Cavies in particular can eat large quantities of grass daily. At the beginning of the year, when the grass is new and fresh, it should be introduced slowly, particularly to young stock, or it will cause scours. Grass clippings should never be fed, as these rapidly heat up and cause scours and bloating.

Ground Elder *(Aegopodium podagraria)*

Description:- This plant is also known as Gout Weed. It is a tenacious weed, and is a creeping medium sized perennial. The leaves are trefoil, and the flowers are white and grow in umbrels and appear between June-August. The plant has a distinctive smell when picked.

Habitat:- Shady and waste places.

Uses:- The leaves can be safely fed, until the flower stems and flowers appear at the beginning of June.

Ground Elder

Groundsel *(Senecio vulgaris)*

Description:- This is a common and well recognised weed. It is an annual, and may grow to a height of 12 inches. The leaves are shaped like little oak leaves, and the flowers are like tiny dandelion flowers. It is in flower all year.

Groundsel

Habitat:- It is a weed of cultivation, and is found in gardens, and disturbed ground.

Uses:- The whole plant may be fed. It should not be used if it is covered in orange mould spots. It is laxative in action, and should be fed sparingly, and in conjunction with astringent plants. It is also useful for encouraging a slow moult. It is also a stimulating tonic, and a rich mineral source.

Knapweed *(Centaurea spp.)*

Description:-   The commonest Knapweed is Black Knapweed. It is a short/medium perennial. The flower heads are purple and similar to a thistle in shape. The long leaves are cut into egg-shaped   segments, becoming simpler as they get closer to the flower head. The stem is covered with soft hairs, not thistles. It flowers between July-September.

Habitat:- Dry waste ground, hedgerows and pastures.

Uses:- The whole plant can be fed. It is astringent in action.

Knapweed

Mallow *(Malva sylvestris)*

Description:- The Common mallow is a familiar hedgerow plant. It is a medium/tall annual/perennial. The flowers are purple, 25-40mm in diameter. The leaves are kidney shaped, often with a small dark spot on them. The Mallow flowers between June-October.

Habitat:- Waste places and waysides.

Uses:- All parts of the plant can be fed, and all species of Mallow can be used. The plant is

Mallow

astringent, and has expectorant properties, useful for conditions of the respiratory system.

Mayweed

There are two species of Mayweed, Scentless Mayweed *(tripleurospermum inodorum)* and Pineapple Mayweed *(matricia matricaioides)*. They are closely related to Chamomile spp.

Description:- Scentless Mayweed is an odourless, hairless annual/biennial. The flowers are daisy-like, 15-40mm in diameter. The leaves are hairlike. It flowers from April-October. Pineapple Mayweed is scented, and the flowerheads are yellow-green, resembling miniature

Pineapple Mayweed

pineapples. It is a short annual. It flowers from May-November.

Habitat:- Bare and waste ground.

Uses:- All parts of these plants can be fed to rabbits. Feed sparingly to guinea pigs.

Scentless Mayweed

Plantain *(Plantago spp)*

There are two types of Plantain. The Greater (broad leaved) Plantain, and Ribwort Plantain.

Description:- Greater Plantain is a low perennial. The leaves are a broad oval shape. The flowers are greenish-yellow in long greenish spikes. It flowers from June-October. Ribwort Plantain is a low/medium perennial. The leaves are long and narrow, and ribbed along the length of the leaf. The flowers are on short black spikes, at the end of long stalks.

Habitat:- Grassy and waste places, paths and lawns.

Uses:- All parts of the plant may be fed. They are a good source of vitamins and minerals, and have astringent and diuretic properties. Plantains are also said to have antimicrobial action, and help the body resist, and fight off, infection.

Broad Leaved Plantain

Ribwort Plantain

Raspberry *(Rubus idaeus)*

Description:- Raspberry grow wild, and cultivated. Similar to the Blackberry, but with smaller flowers, and weaker prickles on the stems.

Habitat:- Shady places, and widely cultivated.

Uses:- Raspberry leaves are astringent. They are however, probably best known for their action on the uterine muscles. Raspberry leaves fed during the last third of gestation are said to lead to easier births. They may also stimulate milk production in lactating sows and does.

Sea Beet *(Beta vulgaris* ssp. *maritima)*

Description:- This is a sprawling hairless perennial. It resembles spinach and is also called 'Sea Spinach'. The stalks are red tinged, and the leaves are dark green. The leaves alternate with the flowers up the stem, and the flowers are green and petalless.

Habitat:- By the coast and on shingle beaches.

Uses:- Rich in nutrients, these are a useful addition to the diet, and the leaves are available most of the year. All parts of the plant can be fed.

Sea Beet

Shepherd's Purse

Sow Thistle

Shepherd's Purse *(Capsella bursa-pastoris)*

Description:- This is a low/medium annual/perennial. The flowers are small and white, and the leaves are long and thin on the stalk, and also form a rosette around the base. The seed pods are characteristic heart-shaped, and purse-like from whence it gets its name.

Habitat:- This is a common plant found on dry waste ground.

Uses:- This is one of the most useful wild plants. All parts of the plant can be fed, and it can be dried to feed during the winter when it is not available fresh. It is astringent and should be given at the first sign of scouring in the stock. It also has tonic properties. It also has a stimulating effect on the womb, and can be used as a first aid measure to help prevent excessive post-partum bleeding.

It should not be used if it has a white fungus on the stem.

Sow Thistle *(Sonchus oleraceus)*

Description:- This plant is also known as Milk Thistle, as when the hollow stem is snapped it exudes a milky substance. Sow Thistle comes in smooth and prickly variations, both types can be fed, the smooth Sow Thistle is most popular.

It is a medium/tall annual, the flowers are yellow and similar to a dandelion head. The leaves are pinnately lobed, with the end lobe being the largest. The leaves clasp the stem with arrow-shaped points. Prickly Sow Thistle has leaves with sharper spines, and they clasp the stem with rounded lobes. Both types flower between June-September.

Habitat:- Bare and waste ground.

Uses:- The succulent stems make this plant an excellent feed for nursing sows and does. It is also enjoyed by stock of any age. All parts of the plant can be fed. The older stems, which become woody, are less palatable.

Trefoil

Trefoil *(Lotus corniculatus)*

Description:- Birdsfoot trefoil is a member of the pea family, similar to Clovers and Vetches. It is a creeping perennial, with yellow flowers, tinged with orange and red. It has long brown seed pods which spread out like a bird's foot, from whence it gets its name. It is also known as 'Eggs and Bacon'. It flowers from May-September.

Habitat:- Waysides and grassy places.

Uses:- A good source of vitamins and minerals.

Vetch *(Vicia spp.)*

Description:- There are many species of vetch, and all can be safely fed. Vetches are members of the pea family, they are clambering perennials and their flowers are similar to small sweet pea heads. The flowers may be red, purple, pink, white and yellow. They flower from June-August. The seed pods are brown and resemble pea pods.

Habitat:- Waysides, hedges, and grassy grounds.

Uses:- All parts of the plant can be fed. They are a good source of vitamins and minerals, and are a useful foodstuff.

Vetch

Wild Strawberry *(Fragaria vesca)*

Description:- This plant is well recognised, being a miniature replica of the cultivated strawberry. It flowers during the summer, and the small red fruits appear from June onwards.

Habitat:- Shady banks and woodlands.

Uses:- In common with the Blackberry and Raspberry, the leaves have astringent properties.

Yarrow *(Achillea millefolium)*

Description:- This is a short/medium perennial, with a downy stem, and a pleasant aroma. The leaves are dark green, and feathery. The flowers are small, either white or pink, and arranged in flat umbrel-like clusters, at the top of tough stems. It flowers from June-November.

Habitat:- Grassy places.

Uses:- Yarrow is another plant with excellent astringent action. It is also diuretic, and is of value as a urinary antiseptic, and can be given in cases of cystitis.

Yarrow

CHAPTER 3
Cultivated Plants and Vegetables

All cultivated vegetables can be fed, to provide a varied diet rich in vitamins and minerals. There is conflicting advice in the literature about potatoes and I do not feed them, raw or cooked. Fruits can also be included in the diet as treats.

The following is not a complete list, but includes the main vegetables available, and comments where appropriate.

Beetroot. Contains folic acid, calcium, iron, sodium and vitamin C (10mg/100mg), also vitamins B1 and B2. Too many leafy tops must not be fed as they contain high levels of oxalic acid which will cause acute renal failure.

Broccoli. Contains vitamins A and B2, folic acid and vitamin C. Both white and purple sprouting varieties can be fed.

Brussel sprouts. The leaves and sprouts can be fed. They are a good source of vitamin C and also vitamins A, B6 and folic acid.

Cabbage. Contains vitamins A and B6, folic acid, and is a good source of vitamin C. It is a moderate source of calcium, also iron, copper and potassium.

Carrot and carrot tops. Contains calcium, iron, sodium and vitamins A, B1, B2, B6 and C.

Celery. Both leaves and stalks can be fed. Contains vitamins A, B1 and C.

Cauliflower. The leaves are nutritionally similar to cabbage. Some rabbits will also eat the white heads.

Lettuce. This should only be fed in small amounts. It contains vitamin C, but also contains the substance laudanum which can be harmful.

Spinach. This contains calcium, iron, sodium potassium and magnesium. It also contains vitamins A, B2, B6, E and C and folic acid.

Swede. This is a reasonable source of vitamin C, but its quality deteriorates during storage as it becomes dry and fibrous.

Watercress. This can be given as a treat. It contains calcium, sodium, vitamins A and C and folic acid.

Fruits

Any fruits can be given as treats. Tomato and banana are good sources of potassium, and are worth considering feeding to weak, floppy rabbits, a condition which may be associated with potassium deficiency.

Kiwi fruits are good sources of vitamin C.

Trees

Rabbits also enjoy the leaves and branches of two trees, Apple and Hazel. Apple trees need no introduction, the leaves can be fed all year, when pruning the trees. Gnawing on the bark keeps the incisors wearing well.

Hazel *(Corylus avellana)*

Native to West Asia, North Africa and Europe, including Britain. It is a deciduous tree, forming bushy thickets up to 20ft high. The leaves are coarse and hairy. It should not be confused with Beech, whose leaves are smoother and greasy.

Hazel

CHAPTER 4
Poisonous Plants

This list of edible plants should give enough variation of foodstuffs to avoid trying any other plants, but the most poisonous plants, together with a few comments are listed below.

All plants that grow from bulbs (Crocus, Bluebell etc.)
Anemones
Arum ('Lords and Ladies')
Bracken
Bryony
Buttercup (although this is safe if small quantities are found dried in hay)
Celandine
Charlock
Convolvulus (Bindweed)
Deadly Nightshade (Belladonna)
Docks once the flowers appear as the woody leaves contain oxalic acid which causes renal failure
Figwort
Flats (Iris spp)
Fool's Parsley
Foxglove - this contains digitalis, a heart stimulant, and symptoms include tremor and fitting. The symptoms may be controlled by administering oral calcium in the liquid form Collo-cal D at a dose of 0.5ml/kg twice daily.
Ground Elder once the flowers appear, as its action then becomes too diuretic.
Hellebore
Hemlock

Henbane

Horsetails

Iris

Lily of The Valley

Monkshood

Oak leaves - these will cause renal failure

Poppies

Privet

Ragwort - this causes fatal liver failure

Scarlet Pimpernel

Speedwell

Spurge

Toadflax ('Old Man's Beard')

Travellers Joy

Wild celery

APPENDIX

Supplements for Rabbits

If a rabbit is on a healthy, well balanced diet there should be no need for supplementation, however, there are some instances where the following products may be useful.

Probiotics

Probiotics contain live beneficial bacteria which can temporarily colonise the gastrointestinal tract. They are useful for protecting the gut flora from *Clostridium spp.* multiplication during antibiotic administration, times of stress, (e.g. weaning) or in cases of sickness, particularly when scouring. They can also be useful appetite stimulants.

A probiotic such as Avipro (Vetark Health) provides *Lactobacillus acidophilus, Enterococcus faecium, Saccharomyces* and electrolytes. The *lactobacillus* is encapsulated, and able to pass through the stomach's acidity into the caecum.

Vitamins and Minerals

These may be a useful supplement for rabbits during growth, breeding and to combat the effects of stress or disease. They also have a place in the prevention of dental disease which may result from the under-mineralisation of the teeth and jaw bones. Care must be taken not to overdose with these powders as there is a risk of causing bladder stones if the calcium content of the diet is too high.

SA37 (Intervet UK Ltd) is a powder that can be sprinkled on the food 2-3 times a week. It is particularly useful for rabbits that selectively leave the pelleted component of their dry food, or those that have dental disease.

Arkvits (Vetark Health) is a similar powder that can be added to the food, daily as necessary.

Boost 250 (Stock Nutrition) is a soluble multivitamin supplement which can be added to the drinking water.

Vitamin C - this vitamin can be given alone to help fight infection. Soluble vitamin C tablets can be dissolved in the drinking water at a dilution of 200mg/litre. Overdosage is not possible as any extra is excreted through the kidneys. It is useful in instances of bladder disease as it can help acidify the urine. It does come formulated with cranberry tablets (Larkhill Green Farm) for this purpose.

Herbal Remedies

There is a vast range of herbal products available for use in rabbits, many based on the plants mentioned in the text, formulated in a dry or powdered form. Further information can be gained from Galens Garden, 62 Castle Avenue, East Ewell, Surrey.

INDEX